NOTES TOWARD A FAMILY TREE

OTHER POETRY TITLES FROM QUARRY PRESS

Homeless Heart
DON BAILEY

Great Men
JOHN BARTON

The Burden of Jonah ben Amittai
ALLAN BROWN

The Year in Pictures
BARBARA CAREY

The Unavoidable Man
BARRY DEMPSTER

Wintering Over
JOAN FINNIGAN

Mating in Captivity
GENNI GUNN

Stalin's Carnival
STEVEN HEIGHTON

Talking Prophet Blues
MAGGIE HELWIG

Why is Snow So White?
F.H. LOW-BEER

The Litmus Body
NADINE McINNIS

The Hummingbird Murders
SUSAN McMASTER

Traveling in the Gait of a Fox
DACIA MARAINI

How To Be Born Again
COLIN MORTON

The Untidy Bride
SANDRA NICHOLLS

In the House of No
KEN NORRIS

The Speed of the Wheel Is Up to the Potter
SANDY SHREVE

Tolstoy at Yasnaya Polyana
GEORGE WOODCOCK

NOTES TOWARD A FAMILY TREE

JOHN BARTON

Quarry Press

The publisher gratefully acknowledges the support of The Canada Council, the Ontario Arts Council, the Department of Communications, and the Ontario Publishing Centre.

Canadian Cataloguing in Publication Data

Barton, John, 1957 —
    Notes toward a family tree

Poems.
ISBN 1–55082–066–4

    I. Title.

PS8553.A78N68 1993   CB11'.54   C93–0,
PR9199.3.B37N68 1993

Cover art entitled *East Hampton Memories* by Rafal Olbinski, reproduced by permission of the artist. Design by Keith Abraham. Typeset by Susan Hannah. Printed and bound in Canada by Best-Gagné Book Manufacturers, Toronto, Ontario.

Published by Quarry Press, Inc., P.O. Box 1061, Kingston, Ontario K7L 4Y5.

for Stephen and Mary

In the slow rise to the self, we're drawn up by many hands.
CHARLES WRIGHT

CONTENTS

1

THE MOON IN ALL ITS PHASES

2

BRANCHES OF THE LARGER FOREST

3
THE WORLD IN DECLINE

1
THE MOON IN ALL ITS PHASES

John Barton

Now that Hiroshima Is Past Us

After the air has cleared and humiliation
has left a film
of fall-out to expose our bones, there is room

to recall how love unfolded

its awful cloud,
how its conspiracy with fate

made waste of our hearts,
of what we can never claim as ours

but still desire.
In Hiroshima there is a man whose lust

evaporated into mist

the moment the bomb fell,
his forehead warping

under his lover's
melting fingers as she died
without enough time

to feel her death

take form,
her fingers burning through
the convolutions

in his mind.
She left him no words

to describe her pain.
In Hiroshima one comes

to love the misshapen lives of men
and women,
and their deformed purpose.
From now on, mine is a lover's ear:

lotus are forever whispering,
forever opening their innocence
to the city's Square of Peace.

For a Moment This

is my dream: to love one
woman, wake

beside her Sunday morning, late,
break inside her like a wave

across a salt-licked beach,
bright stones

caught in its crest
like stars

eroding the night-flared sky.
Then a simple breakfast:

coffee, croissants, grapefruit,
sitting together in a sun-

filled window, CBC on,
Gilmor's Albums, old Clyde rambling on

about Mahler or Sarah Vaughan,
the radio switched off

before the news at 1:00.
Once dressed, an hour's walk.

We take bread for the ducks,
winter-starved and nudging

their bills into our
expectant palms.

At The Delta's Edge

Your mind is a clever house
precariously pitched
on stilts at the delta's edge.
With the other mammoths
of your imagination
I am pinned by its bamboo foundations.
My muscles tense under the weight
of sediment filtering
to the river bottom.

I feel the house arrange your heart's
furnishings with a Chinese restraint.
There a scroll on a certain summer wall.
There an ebony seat looking
through a certain evening window at the geese.
Harmony, you always said,
requires devotion.
You kept a single orchid
in a slender vase on your bedside table.
Once we broke from sleep to find it
shattered on the floor.
Certain I had knocked it with my hand
you could not speak.
All week you repaired without a word
its order: what you thought
a flawless vision of man and woman
you restored to antique perfection
except for a single piece.
How often in the starlight
draining from your eyelids
did I puzzle over that proud man
missing half his face?
Now I wonder if you feel
snaking down his torso, each crack
adding refinement to the glaze.

Someday I want to rise through
the river surface,
the accretions of time I am wearing
one by one washed away.
You would find me waiting
in the shallows outside your door,
elemental as a member of a tribe
discovered by chance
outside the jungle's untouched heart,
my urgency modern
as all eternal things.
I would tell you
the moon in all its phases
beats behind my ribs.
It tells me I would break
your body's slender vase
and fill you
again and again.

Another man's step radiates
through your lacquered floor
tonight.
              I can feel his heat.
I can feel the slow
web of his fingers lightly
tangle in the lines
opening across your face and hands,
each line a thread of stars.
I touch you with his hands.
Looking at the palms
I wonder at all that can fall
through the constellations
two lovers weave,
love a comet
chance and slippery as a seed.

My Favourite Green Sweater

my favourite green sweater is in her
mind
          it is folded
over a kitchen chair, the left sleeve
dangling
to the floor, all day
she wore it for warmth, but
now that she is at
home alone, she sits in the chair
opposite and smokes, watching the grey
sun swim across her yellow
table, watching my green sweater
recede into the kitchen's
ink dark

The Reverse Side of a Picture Postcard

I practised packing my suitcase last night,
wrinkled every shirt folding them down,
pulled out all I plan to leave behind
from what I always keep.   Here's a toothbrush
I have never used.   I never broke its magic
seal of cellophane. Already I imagine how
its bristles are meant to touch your lips
unfelt. Watching you comb your hair once
in the mirror above your sink, I lay back
in limbo on your bed and noticed the formula
Chinese fortune taped above your reflected face.
Its poetry will not keep you safe. The soul
leaves the body the same way every night,
comes back in the same way I would have
entered you as you wake, a vision
you don't want. You are afraid its music
will fizz like sodas your father bought you
when you were eight on trips to Memphis
before he died. Such music you feel
will trick you by going flat at any time.
Our only kiss winds through you
like a pre-recorded tape. You've tried
re-wind, fast-forward, pause, now *erase*.
I'm not there while you talk on the phone
to Asheville, Little Rock, to God above
who chucked me out of heaven long before we met.

I'm not there while you say *You can't leave me*
to a man in another state whose love-name
I will not remember years from now
if I run into you by chance in the dark
passages that connect us while we sleep.
I was already gone the first time
you steeled yourself to hug me gently
good-bye once when I took off
downtown to shop, the subway token
you lent me jangling with the change
in my jeans. Racing down flights of stairs
I was already slipping from you,
the nights sucking me into the starless
mazes that burn hypnotically beneath Manhattan.

Straits of Juan de Fuca

Looking back, the land fell away
first.   Closing on themselves
like a trap, the headlands melted one
into the next until all were flat,
razor-edged against the chalk dawn.
Leaving by water I did not notice

and notice only now how a certain
seawall walk we took —
the fall air chafed with burning
leaves and salt — elucidates
that coast, the stone beneath us
so cold it defied the ocean's force.

We lent our bodies to the masoned rail,
leant into hollows left by other elbows.
To hold you took a week.
As we talked you casually smoked and said:
I have time for beauty now,
then turned my collar against the wind.

I look back from this other shore.
Mountains whose edges I am weighing down
tip up like shells dropped by ravens.
Words we said remain snagged like tufts
of mist in their ragged peaks.
At sea level you told me about *Snow Country,*

another novel by Kawabata I have never read,
the heat of his lodge offered up
in your wind-red face.   *Bank the coals,*
your eyes said, *close the door.*
Now I know how numb lovers can be to snow,
risk temporary deaths falling into what they sense

is each other's warmth.
That day we were too busy, too dangerously mortal
against the ocean's fiery gold
to notice what wreckage hung in lighted depths.
Even now the ferry I caught here
polishes over this unfathomed cache, shuttling

back and forth like a bead
on an abacus I once fingered to keep account.

Six Letters in Autumn and One Unwritten

1

A year since the last October moon.

A year since we were tenants
in different
beds with the same woman.

Yet the nights were full.
Nights of laughter rising

from her,
palpable under our different hands.
Laughter lightly shed —

chestnut threads
pulled through her moonlit hair —

washes of harvest
through the sky's unexpected silk.

2

Today,
just as the flame tree
broke into final flower,
I lost the poem you left
last year in the mail box
with my other bills.
The entry light,
a small moon, intense
with ivy, with moths,
sent wings of shadow
light tumbling
like leaves, like angels
through my door.
Inside your poem her
laughter woke.
Woke brightly —
light fingers turning
my dead bolt deftly,
its chamber soundless
the whole building soundless,
until slender nails cut
through shadows draping
your only window.
That night you were
lying between
sheets of darkness,
dark eyes open.
You felt us
spinning madly
through your thoughts,
spinning laughter into
a web so thin
we fell through.

Later you watched
us fall singly,
our half-sprouted wings
melting into the moon's
blank clock face.
I can imagine
your helplessness
for months, for hours.
Impossible to imagine
me falling even now.

3

These months I have felt the moon's
repetitions
fruit inside my ribs.

Each month these fingers
stumbled
through this heart's breviary of useful prayers

and found all recurring newness
sour.

Found illumination.
Illumination —

I asked you for knowledge.
You offered me time,
and with eyes laughing,

the erosion of time.

4

FROM A NIGHT JOURNAL

only wrong is done in the telling
                RAINER MARIA RILKE

At last November.
At last All Soul's Day.
The day of the dead,
nights falling through
webs of branches
clattering dry leaves.

Outside my window
the elms settle for
the wind's embrace.
Inside, music.
Notes and a voice
dropping
into pools of rain.

Stephen phoned last night.
His words opened
around me in rings.
I jumped through them
with news, with laughter.
What else could I say?

In a dream last night
I was water
sinking through rings
in a great tree.
Tonight at my table
I started counting rings
my glass made on the oak.
I was writing Stephen
a letter.
I threw it away.

I can read such want
in a leaf
turning to night
or in a face.

I can read this want.
Easily
I can learn to turn it
away.

But in my blood,
in my face,
in the face draining
of light
in any mirror that catches
my eye, angrily

I sense in my blood
leaves falling,
falling unnamed.

Like the moon a tree
in winter glances
off the sun, its crown
of naked branches
a vacated room.

In his voice last night
such unnoticed harvest.
I have gathered his words
like leaves for hours
hung them on my heart's
crooked branches.
They smile.

5

To define loss the moon
opens the sky,
nightly spilling its hoard
of stars snagged
into nets.
They trawl the dark,
pull from its undertow
breath: the night
wind suspended
in calm.
Last spring I was walking
home by the sea,
breakers breaking,
recollecting,
then breaking again.
Reflections deepened.
Stars threw themselves
into the dark.
In the moonlight
the planets aligned.
Whole histories,
future and past,
personal and man's,
hung in a pause,
shone like wet
newborn about to
drop from the womb.
High on those cliffs,
all I can be,
all I was,
aligned briefly,
all details knotting
simply, gently
into one story.
The planets themselves
drew apart.

Something was erased.
As I walked on
I couldn't imagine time
had ever broken
its step — yet
as I write this
I know in imagination
I will not always
be walking,
will not always
be on my way home;
I know one day
I will open the door —
that night for instance
such harvest,
though I soon felt
myself forgetting
its grasp,
as a seed forgets,
grappling with soil,
the sketch of a tree
inside it
completing the sky.
Even now I feel
that night still
leaving its structure,
like warmth
on the skin
from a withdrawing hand —
as a blank sky does
the new moon's secret
incubation of light;
as the heart does
love's unfurling ensigns —
leaves in bud
on branches of blood.

6

After the moonlight's haphazard
fall, slivering

the ocean's skin
with such unaccountable

fragments,
this was unexpected:

I have abandoned explanation.
With the same facts

you tacked together
a different story just as moot.

With the same unpractised hands
we touched

a different woman,
though, like me, you let her

leave countless times,
though only once finally,

and for different reasons.
For different reasons, finally

you stopped counting,
as I stop counting, slowly,

each time the moon grows
full

beneath our heads,
though the days are beads.

7

Since you left I have remembered
the minutiae of your face
and hands, lifted debris
from every bore as a smith would
dints from a silver cup.
You are constantly reborn.

Here we are, and were,
two men meeting for the first
time over coffee and talk,
watching leaves gracefully
snake to the earth;
and later, in a midnight cove,
hunched up on driftwood
one Christmas, the two of us
resting elbows on knees,
shivering, our two lives
opening like an iron gate,
shore mist blurring the waves;
and still later, in a bar,
flipsides of the same woman,
a game of hesitance and remorse,
jazz, laughter, the waitress
caught in our forced
lightness like a moth;
and still later, in your kitchen,
the day after she left me,
two months after she left you,
your hand on my shoulder,
your face dark against pale
morning light, your voice
exhausted, restrained,
smoke twisting from a flame;

and finally, the day you left,
your hand on my shoulder,
your foot one foot from the gas,
my face a contusion of loss,
anger, and tears as you held me,
thinking of the long climb
into the interior mountains,
coal towns and money to earn,
brook trout and distance.

I am not alone here healing.
A woman down the street
reads in a window on sun-marked
days drinking tea, and looking
away from her book, can spur
me to laughter, saying her last man
made himself an unwritten letter,
an unopened letter.
How often have her eyes
and mine illumined the rain,
the moon in its last crescent,
the two of us home from the sea?
And another, a friend I shelve
books with at work,
keeps shuffling his cards,
a royal flush yet to flesh out,
a full house of want—
both of us at times
so desperate for love
we open our lives
warmly near the windows,
shafts of light
falling, row after row,
between the dark
knowledge of books.

Such a gift this art
of healing, of growing still,
changing like a leaf
aware on an unfurling self.
Despite our words of anger
I have kept much —

your eyes quiet
each time we broke bread
in my kitchen
while outside the ivy
quaked in the wind;

your eyes holding mine
quietly, the eyes
of the woman ours followed,
spinning, talismanic with loss;

and though sometimes
you could not understand,
and sometimes, laughing,
would not admit to
the moon's recurrent circuit of pain,

your eyes quietening
each time you said my name.

In the Year of

This is not the woman you met
on the great jade steps
of the Imperial Palace Museum.
That woman you talked of
only once, then she was lost,
left among the loot of China;
a figure stopping a moment
on a staircase, a lacquered gate,
your smile and too few words.

Who is this? This woman
shy beside you at my door?
Yet another from the same
tumid summer in Taiwan?
One more of those who fell
so briefly down beside you,
so gently into the scented
sheets of several afternoons?

This one does not seem yet
a lover. She does not yet
take your hand and count
each finger as if distracted.
Arranged on the couch arm so
modestly beside you she stares
at the odd trees coming
into leaf against my window.
Half aloud she wonders
if such trees bear fruit.

She must be the one
I have long expected.
The one you obliquely mentioned.
The one who stepped from
behind a screen of air
at a bus stop and gave you
the right directions.

In a picture I once saw
of you, you are sitting
with one arm around her
on a terrace spread
above the snaking heat
of streets in old Taipei —
your glance toward the lens
a rising thread of incense.

Right now your untangling gaze
is wound up in the movements
of her hands. Resting two fingers
a moment below one breast,
she studies the clouds
fret across the deepened sky.
She notices the Ming designs
billowing through the curtains.
Quietly she begins explaining
the good luck of the peach,
the peasant meaning
of its slight heart shape.

Saltspring

"the price of pain is love"
                    ELIZABETH SMART

Just anchored by the cold dawn
a tent of darkness
lists near a table presided over
by crows, set for breakfast
by our late night drinking:
beer and old cheese,
candles burned down to three
stubby white fingers,
the wax dull
in the scars of the wood.

Inside the tent your brother
sleeps with an old lover
he met in the local
by chance. He lost her
five years before
as she was losing herself.
Last night they were found.
This morning, long fallen
asleep, they are in
no hurry to wake.

While you dream deeper
into the beginning
of day, I am looking out
to islands risen
in the gulf between us
and the mainland
where we have for a time
left women real and imagined,

our winter just passed,
the year's blossoming directions,
its half-formed fruit already
heavy in our fingers' anxious grasp.

This island preserves
what we have brought with us
in its marshes of salt.
Over one year of wanting this
sharing we have
seals for a moment the heart
free of its record of loss,
the wax forever holding
inside us words we add to,
words we exchange like baseball
cards again and again.

Last night by the fire
you told me the stars above us
join us, their light still
ours should our orbits
ever turn us apart.
And I agree.
Life's axis is tilted
by such stases in time.

This morning makes this island
my heart, its darkness
receding into blue
sky and sun hidden by cloud.
The first beams ease through
like new shoots.

I want to shake you awake,
share with you an instant
where crows wondrously feed
on our leavings and
lovers make themselves stars
however brief.
    I let you be.
Sweat shines on your face.
You too have strenuous dreams
hoeing a space clear
in your heart.
No longer can we each simply be
squatters in our private selves.
We must claim the land.
Dear friend, we must begin
seeding our fallen
stars in the soil.

2
BRANCHES OF THE LARGER FOREST

Ghost River

Before the dam was built
the river was a whisper.
                Sixty years later
as children
my sister
and I camped on the lakeshore. No one
heard how the river
crept past,

how the dam sent it
back on itself,
swallowing the hills that skirted
its path.

But no one worried.
Moments after our father's car slid
down to the beach,
                I let the cold water
take my breath away as I sank
to snare minnows with a net.
For my sister, older, my family
favourite and just
offshore,
        it was breathtaking
how the lake forever held
the mountains as they stretched
into the sunset

ringing her thighs.
Already the man who took her

from me was forming in her eyes.
A man simpler than a mountain pool
who already held her
clearly in his mind.
Those we love are ghosts

we project into the future.
They rise from the lake bottom

at the appointed hour.
Ten years later my sister met
her man.
           The wetness
of their bodies
pools even now in the hollows
of their bed.

The Centrepiece

"I can call nothing love that does not answer."
                    PHYLLIS WEBB

Many years we sat opposite
one another at supper
as before a mirror
and with as much comfort
between the antipodes of the earth,
mother and father,
and how they argued.

We always threatened
to buy them a centrepiece
that would stretch to the ceiling,
a tangle of branches
words couldn't fly through.
Instead we acquiesced
in Mum's summer perennials
and winter's everlastings.
That was our parents' sense
of surviving, of not doing,
and they passed it on —
a legacy wordless
as the wisdom teeth
we later had removed.

How many dinners did we sit through,
our eyes blurred
by the slow rhythm of our forks
from plate to mouth,
the bland stratagems of the words
that he carved and she served
exploding into silence
and dessert?

Being older you may have felt more
as your body began taking
a distinct shape beneath your dress,
six years before my shoulders
broadened.
It was in your eyes then,
though I see it only now.

Already your heart was forming
words that would excuse
you from the table,
words you slipped away with
before I began silently
to pack my books.
Only now do we see they paused
to watch us leave.
We refused to notice.
There was nothing we could do.

And now we find them
dividing the effects of forty years
between them like a cell,
the two of us required
only now to fill the gap
habit has set between us,
a conversation without centre.
Your elbow resting on the table
while you watch, I pour
us each a glass of wine,

remark on the concentration
of your gaze, an active
blue clarity that sits down
between us and laughs,
serves us what we need.

In My Twenty-Fifth Year

I am forever seven,
eating tuna fish sandwiches
at our yellow kitchen
table with my mother,
the window framing
us with grey prairie rain.
This is the mud season
before spring. Soft light
blurs the robins' return,
the steady growth of
shadow lengthening
from the brevity of noon.
Then the air
breaks into song.
Right now only a discord
of winter sparrows choirs
in our back garden trees.
No matter how far the roots
send shoots fingering
for warmth in the earth,
no matter how roughly
leafless branches scissor
a path through the clouds,
the sun will come out only
when it wants. Just as I
in a few minutes will
drink the last inch of milk
my mother poured into
my glass. Just as she
will finish the dregs
of her quickly brewed tea.

We sit awhile longer,
savour what is left of this
lunch my mother has made
time for. The salty tuna
is sweet on my tongue.
The light of this room
leaks in through cracks
in my twenty-fifth year.
I find myself listening
to bare branches
thrumming glass before dawn.

Patterns

Bifocals hang against his chest.
My father watches the siskins
outside the window crack seeds,
scatter husks across the flowerbeds.
Quicksilver wings throw back
triangles of sudden morning
light as they scatter,
settle in far-off branches.

I settle behind him in a chair pulled
from the tight circle of the kitchen table,
my face sketched in by what sun
filters round his shoulders.

Next to him stands the grandfather clock
that cast shadows down the hall
of my parents' house before he left.
The persistence of its chime
increased by the hour.
Through the years it chimed
off-sync with the mantle clock
my mother wound up on her desk.
I fell asleep between them
in the room passed down from child
to child, shadows
left behind like husks.
My sisters fell asleep between
that brooding rivalry of bells.
Did they, like me, seldom
wake to quiet?

It is quiet now.
Moving house, the old granddad
has lost its tongue,
its monologue not flushed out
by wedges my father
shoved beneath falcon-toed feet
at an attempt for balance.
My stepmother dusts
the still, arthritic
hands and pallid face.

I too have changed,
hair thinning, body tired
of moving; the ache of finding
comfort scattered
in the arms of far-off
cities has consumed my days.
Here for the weekend,
I pull myself up beside this
man who remains always
two inches taller,
recognize myself, his silence.

We look out, my mother
an unspoken word between us,
an alarm we let run down
like the egg timer
when she made us breakfast.

We look out, watch the clutch
of siskins wheel and scatter,
wings sustaining a net
of shapes against the sun.
I reach out.
The window opens,
birdsong a knot that slips undone
in flight, pulled
taut like love when at last
it settles.

Notes Toward a Family Tree

Inside you while you sleep
a shadow
spreads like shade
under a baobab tree in late
evening sun,
                    its umbrella
of contorted
branches pendulous with
fruit.
            Sprawled
in the tree's arms
a lion yawns.
                    With night
the shade spreads,
touches the entire
inside of your skin,
stains it black —
the blackness native
drums,
            a jackal's
yammer, the ache
of a negro
woman giving birth.

In the morning you appear
to wear your white
skin with little effort,
having learned the ease
of northern light
in your mother's house.
While I set your table
you tell me
of the pearl-handled knives
she gave you
knotted neatly in silk,
hidden with her letters
in a dresser drawer.

Lazing in a chair
you smooth your skirt.
Only when your husband's
left for town to shop
do I see the daughter
you will never conceive
move slightly beneath
your breasts.
        Husband,
I can sometimes
hear stirring in the missed
beats of your orphaned
heart, *may I always*
know your hands
warm on my stomach.
        Daughter,
may I always dress
your hair with shells
I gathered on the sandbars of our mother Congo.

I would ask you

how many bodies
do we carry
unborn.
  Mothers,
fathers,
   cathartic
lovers,
  dreams
of the self that spin
forever
inside us,
each a compass
without hands
or face?

I would ask you
how many.

I would ask you
how many more
directions
must we conceive.

Each destination
never quite
arrived at, a continent
never quite
cut loose from
the mind's
idea of grace.

I would ask you
all this,
        perhaps even
more,

        (What might have grown there?
         What impossible tree?)

but sitting on your
porch,
the sky unrolling behind
the crooked arms of your arbutus
a diagram of unfinished stars,
all things seem

unaccountable, uncountable,
and in our life-

times, timeless, and without

name.

I would tell you

of origins,
the mathematics of sight —
the pupil
a point where the arc of one leaf curving
to earth meets
with another's, crosses its path.

I would tell you
we are all children

conceived like this
under the same skin,

leaves loosened
from the same tree.

I would tell you
before my words

fade, slip like bare
branches
into the night,

but the earth's skin
has torn slightly
as the axis strains,

is already turning
us out

of the day.
We are blind mostly,
blind moments of light falling

uncharted through space.

Yet I am led back always
to my first measures:
the plains breaking
against mountain,
the swells frozen
into hills
brown with summer;
in January, cottonwood
branches cottony
with snow, the smallest
twigs a frost
lace drawn closed
across the sky's blue
window.
        Here I learned
passion's cold
roots.
        Here I learned
each tree's promise
of leaves
furled all winter
in black
untended soil.

I return there always
in imagination.

In imagination all
spring I have
watched myself grow.

Now in your face
sometimes I see
my face,
the same sunlit birch
leaf budding once
more into its cut edges
of light,

to fall,

gracefully you say,

once more into the dark's

welcoming

eye.

Alright then.
Though there are no possible gifts,
these are my gifts.

A mirror wrought from tin from a Biafran tomb.
Your face caught in its slant.

Beads.
Snake-ribs for your arms.
A red jute headband
made by your hands.

Your skin is still white though.
This I cannot change.

And for a daughter
I give you your shadow.

She is sleeping
under a baobab tree in a basket twisted
from reeds.
                    In the branches
the moon fattens,
like bread-fruit, on its own light.

In the distance a lioness
calls to her mate.

Love this daughter
for too soon she will grow.

>   (Sister, I live in the next
>   village.
>   As I walked
>   on foot
>   closer to my bed
>   a python
>   forked its tongue at the crossroad.
>   My head restless on my pillow
>   of straw,
>   already I make your girl
>   stay small in my heart.
>   Though she will grow,
>   to me she must always
>   wake as a child.)

In your own way
you will give her the knives
of your mother.

You will give her in song
the warm hands of your husband.

In your own way
you will give her blackness a story,
a penetrable name.

Magnificat

Leaning back into a gossip chair,
the porch window framing her
thoughts with a harvest moon,
her body overwhelmed by a first child —
the father in the basement intuiting
the form of a cradle from dark
maple responding to his hands —
she finds herself growing
light-headed with earlier men.

The husband she made a friend,
the erotic the seed he planted.

The blond lover who grew hard
each time her tongue hesitated
a moment too long exploring
the pit of his left knee,
whose embraces roused her nipples
to unusual swollen peaks,
can still make her flush,
the very thought of him enough.

Another with more gentle eyes,
that held her longer she made
her teacher. They exchanged
books by Thomas Merton,
discussed Krishna and Piaget,
lived several platonic weeks
beneath a mountain.

Still another she imagines
the way she met him, his frame
caught a moment in light enticed
through vines that reach skyward
against a window in his flat,
his hand curved in what for her
became a reflective wave.
Irony, laughter, empathic darkness
she reckoned among his virtues.
Absently she fingers the shirt
he gave her from his closet.
What shape it took stretched
by his chest, buttoned
across a heart she came to doubt,
no longer limply hugs her;
its folds keep her warm,
flare around the baby's
final dream.

The carpenter whose whistling
rises through her bones
like notes will soon lay down
his level and his plane. Only night
allows them time to jest
about the stalk they one day
found creeping up inside her.
These days it seems impatient
to poke its head above the clouds.
They have agreed to let it climb
where it must, though her gaze
must inform its leaves,
his canny touch its tendrils.

Last night in the light falling
between the curtains he showed her
the clever animals he's practised
dancing madly across the walls.
She told him what she read
waiting for him to climb in
beside her. He delighted in mounting
with her the ladder the foetus
ascends from fish to child.

She hears his step rising
from the basement. Soon his eyes
will rest on her like a hand.
For nights now she has dreamed
about the body she will wear again
for him — the baby's almost one
of them, this in-dwelling form
they will find a name for.

Heavenly Bodies

Two eyes dilate in the mirror
hanging from the crib slats
as he rolls closer, stretches
hands tiny and sure
as moths intent on the sun.
Across the room your body,
separate and siphoned of milk,
sinks back into the sofa's
delicious cool silk.

Against the window, the shape
of your five year old
poses with fifteen barrettes in her hair,
ornament for her wedding
to a baby whose eyes have
yet to centre on her.
The hem of her nightie snags
on warped floorboards like a train.
You make her a spray of paper flowers,
whisper husbands
come and go; brothers are forever.

Your husband re-enters the room,
hands you apple
cake on a chipped plate.
Thanks are accepted silently;
his eyes leaving yours
to light on the crib.
In fractions he comes and goes,
thoughts wandering
in conversation, shared at random
or through the many
languages of the body joined
in love or sprawling across an armchair,
his lap roomy enough for the pretend bride
nursing joy and confusion like a bouquet.

Lying back on the couch
with a book you look up from,
you know the front door lock
turns under his touch,
the key-chain you gave him
a charm he keeps in his pocket.

The breeze through an open
window pulls all eyes to the moon
and satin stars tangled over the crib.
You want the future to hold more
and less for your children,
threads crossing and uncrossing,
each heavenly body moving
into a more companionable orbit.
The baby's eyes loll in the mirror.
What he sees there against the changing
blur of the room
is where you want him to begin,
eyes that are human
ears, nose, hands capable of reach.

Housebound

It isn't virtue that makes him
wash the dishes piled
high by others round the pantry sink;

God knows, he'd rather climb
toward some peak in the Coastal Range,
muscles hardening against granite and the fear

of falling, his protection failing,
the utter gravity
of the chasm he dreams he must risk

snapping the fickle ropes that tethered
him unexpectedly to this world.
Instead, through a small

pane of glass he scavenged,
fitted during a free
moment into the chained front door,

he eyes the mountains crystallizing
through mist shining across the inlet;
the dish rag his left hand clenches

drooling soapily on the mat.
Crooked in his arm, his colicky infant squints,
whimpers, and pulls his whiskers,

her discomfort drawing him back down the passage
until the half-light
of a midwinter kitchen appears

to soothe her;
the rice porridge whose secret he's perfected
belches in its happy pan.

The hours calve little transformation;
the days seem to eddy past.
Who knows what form of man will one day slip

through the hands determining this household
a coiled rope
hanging in his troubled grasp?

Topographics

Uncertain of his bearings his mother posts
him maps, shaking her head at this
child forever waylaid at some far-fetched
transfer point beyond her
womb: Winnipeg train station, Marrakech.

Though his letters hunger for brandied fruit cakes
tucked in foil, cushioned
for the journey in styrofoam chips
she cannot shake the image of an alien
body plumping a sleeping bag lost in New York.
Electric razors, cameras, hiking boots, a Seiko watch —
nearly every charm she gives him
he reports missing, phantom gifts elusive in pawn shops.

In a dream she sees his eyes blaze,
a suicide bomber exploding through a checkpoint in Beirut.
Waking, she almost gives up.

But maps furled in mailing tubes like semaphore flags. . .
her baby the centre
of some universe gravely unequipped
with parallels, sources, and marked barrier reefs.

The world she has surveyed for him
unscrolls across his desk.
The Queen Charlotte Islands list in a sea
of contour lines and quantified depths
before he folds the archipelago
against the creases she has tenderly ironed out,
the map stashed beneath letters
from the men he has loved, from the women.
Cancelled stamps are the only *Baedeker* he trusts.

It has taken him years to travel
blind, to move on touch and smell,
cities, like clams, freshest when dug up by chance.

He would prefer to remain helpless
in the wet jungle of some lover's legs and arms
but each river yet to be explored inside him
drains into a day he cannot remember,

the day his mother first let go,
infant feet flatfooting it down a zig-
zag path before he fell
ass-backward toward this world.

Vancouver Gothic

This house is an attempt to make the family nuclear free.
Though a mother and father
stand at the centre.
And though not my parents their love is explosive.
Vancouver gothic: Mary holds Anna
on her hip like a sack of groceries
bought at the health food store down Commercial Drive;
Tom ties on a carpenter's apron,
sawdust mats his hair.
They meet at the kitchen doorway;
they are about to have words.

Down the hall Stephen has been half awake all morning,
lying in bed, unwilling to take a leak;
it's too much work
to stumble to the bathroom and the sheets are so warm.
In a few hours he will close the book
of new age mystics he dozes over,
rise, relieve himself, begin to pump iron.

I sit in the living room and down pots of tea
or close myself into the study,
write letters to those of us already moved down east.
A vanguard before us they take their chances
with opportunity, exile, and grief.
Often I stir a pot of soup I concoct from scraps for lunch
(tomato, mushroom, sometimes beet) and I wait.
Vapours clean the windows and the stock clarifies,
but seldom the reasons why some of us stay.

Refugees from unemployment we divvy up welfare cheques.
We sit in the dining room and divide
equally the costs of our living
here in this wind-razed house where somehow we feel
the world, inner and outer, does not impinge.
Back and forth, Anna our modern day abacus,
skitters under the table
between us, demanding and portioning love.

Through a cracked window sun breaks across a Chinese rug
worn from use, unfurled over damaged floors.
Loose thread snagged between delighted fingers
Anna scuttles ahead of Stephen or Tom.
The pattern ravels.
Even under this uneasy shelter of warped laths
and flaking paint, we make
room for comic relief.
Though unlike laughter rain falls,
collects in buckets in the four corners of the living room,
moves debris into deltas of the cordillera.

Saint Francis of the Passmore

Being reticent he is easy
with stray cats and Karl Marx.
Slipping through the creaking
red door into the shadowed
chaos of the courtyard,
the dialectic mewing
greedily at his feet,
two bowls of milk balanced
in one hand, he smiles,
certain of small things.

Just home from the grave
yard shift, the Saturday
sun catches him unprepared.
Out of habit he shields
his eyes. Years of want
nourish the irony ripening
inside the cage that ribs
slowly knit; the heart an apple
condensing on the tree of blood —
his mother, his father dead;
one brother drowned,
the rest — wind-blown seeds.
Silently he laughs.
Deep eyes follow each twist
of ivy snaking over white
tenement walls into light
and warmth. He has read
nothing stills the heart.

It is almost noon.
Around him twenty bodies singly
stir in thirteen beds,
latecomers to the lightened
silence of waking thoughts.
Above his head a little girl
mumbles TV jingles
while she cleans her teeth.
An old man, windows dark
with thirty years nicotine,
shambles out his door,
a weeks garbage cradled
in his arms
                    That your cat?
He has asked a thousand times.
Deaf, he needs no answer.

Watching two men laugh
through an ivy-draped window
I start to dress.
A woman I love links
her hands round my waist,
unzips my pants.   We laugh.
The day is ours.
The old man creaks back
through his door. The other
crouches among the strays,
two milk-bowls almost empty.
One hand rests gently
on a whiskered, contented head.
The day too is theirs.

The Moabitess

Perhaps the self-same song that found a path
  Through the sad heart of Ruth, when, sick for home,
    She stood in tears amid the alien corn.
                                    JOHN KEATS

Such a strange harvest this house —

it sits inside her, opening.

                    A door.   A window.

Outside maple leaves
rest
the heavy sun on their flushed tips.
She drifts

into a chair, settles.
Her face is damp
from work.
Flesh-
toned lace empties
and swells.
Empties.   Gently swells.
A finger marks a line across the sill.

                    I have come this far.

Pollen on her nail.

My dahlias are just in bloom.

All day she baked her children
bread.
       All day
she counted loaves,
throaty notes of geese fading,
shells gathered in her linen drawer.
All day
she waited.   Wrote letters.

   I have baked the children bread.
   My dahlias bloomed.

In the evening light the table was corn
yellow.

For ten years she kneaded her husband
sourdough.
      In ten years two
children in her
belly rose
to his touch.

     Blessed be his salt.

Now against the window her woman's
face
is dark yet soft.
        Soft against the sun's
flush through the laden

branches of the larger forest.

1475 Fort Street

Not an enclave these rooms
where I live now.
They let in light
through windows that always
look out to
cherry blossoms open
to the first breath of spring.
As I fall asleep
in a bed of my own making
the lie of my parents' house
stretches inside me like a dream
I find I am waking.
Our dog slept
tail curled round snout
in a box outside my door,
under the room where I slept
well as a child.
This room is cool.
I am listening to the dog snore.
I am gritting my teeth.
I am sixteen.
Upstairs my parents are talking.
Their voices are low.
I am glad.
Their voices can only give
shape to the dark.
I turn on my light.
Its shadow raises the ceiling
to where it belongs.
Outside the wind glitters
with frost blowing
off the hills to the north.
Outside a train calls,
reminds me where the river lies
calm as it uncurls.

The tracks running upstream
lead me into the dark
of where I am now.
I turn on my light,
sit in the window until dawn
and remember I woke
to my mother's heels
hard against tile as she
carried dishes from
cupboard to table.

The lie of my parents' house
is the ache my father
felt losing his rib,
the eyes of the woman he found
himself waking beside
turning from his.
She was afraid.
She baked him apples
filled with raisins.
He didn't like them.
Children
fell from her womb.
The rooms where I live
are orphans of pain,
rivals in love,
strangers to trust.
I've seen enough.
I let their dust settle
in the light
of this window where I have sat
all afternoon watching
cherry blossoms open.
Pollen falls from stamen
to pistil off the thighs
of a bee.

The sun is a golden
plum I remember
biting into as a boy
leaning over the steps
to my grandmother's garden
one brilliant afternoon.
I never offer it to
just anyone.
               Taste it.
I find its light delicious
in your throat.

3
THE WORLD
IN DECLINE

Woman in a Nightdress

What woman stands in a nightdress at E53rd and Lex?
I rise out of the subway;
with the crowds that divide around her I walk toward her,

begin to skirt the shaft of afternoon sun that falls over her
like a cage, its bars
the gleaming storeys of sun-resistant glass through which no one

looks — hearts crazed by office politics,
love affairs, and the children's grades.
At street level, we note and try to ignore

the woman's upraised arm, blue-white as ice,
stationary above a head
that quavers like a gyroscope about to loose speed,

chin drawn down toward some uncentred
centre of gravity stuck between half-hidden breasts,
black hair a rag with stray threads hanging.

How at this corner did she come to rest?
Why doesn't she snap her long fingers,
an East Side contessa flagging down a taxi,

her destination mirrored in the surprised eyes
of the driver who would take her a few blocks
further on the journey through whatever city her mind travels?

She haunts us, poised beside us on the curb,
waiting, it seems, for some other light to change.
What signal, inner or outer, will make her cross,

join the blissful anonymity calming this Midtown crowd?
She just stands there with her arm upraised,
Miss Liberty without her torch.

You think it's easy to stand here with my arm
rigid above my head, fingers spread,
palm ignored like a stop sign at this corner

of carefree sales clerks and mothers flaunting prams,
Madison Avenue types tumbling off
buses with Gucci trenchcoats and portfolios flapping.

Cars and bicycles are nimble fish;
laughter zeros
in from all directions, the air smudged

with exhaust and hotdogs half eaten, grabbed on the run.
Balancing here demands patience:
I am a Zen Master, disciplined as anyone

can be in a nightdress stolen
on a madcap
spree through Lord and Taylor one Valentine's Day with Frank.

Fuchsia translucence faded and stained,
flaring slightly in the breezes the crowds make,
my skirt unfurls and furls about me,

some vampish flag I wore to claim him,
a parachute dropping me down to this sunny corner
where I am stopped but not stopping traffic.

Such inertia scares us, the standing still
and growing slowly
more empty and alone, eyes devoid of ambition thrown

back at us by boutique windows and shiny bowls drained
of cafe au lait during our business lunch
or after our visit to the Museum of Natural History,

those dinosaurs immovable, stiffly held erect by ligatures of wire;
each cage of ribs harbouring a vacancy
where long ago nature wound down an uncomprehending heart.

Even the reassuring rhythms of our lungs seem transitory.
The skeletons that carry us through night and day
we imagine stripped of complicit flesh.

Millennia from now some force may expose us,
bone by unarticulated bone, peeling back
unsettling layers of Hudson River waste.

What trouble these hands get me into,
one transfixed above my head,
the fluid fingers of the other congealed into a fist

stuck among the limp folds of this nightdress.
A lullaby Mother would sing
told me that I held the whole world in my hands,

tiny palms abraded by the fictions of its uncontrollable spin —
news reports and sibling feuds I was never equal to,
my entire life a top wobbling on a slow axis.

With these hands I tried to think,
confusing left and right, good with bad.
With these hands I understood nothing.

Without my asking, they began to voice my needs,
rifling the maid's closet or Father's wallet,
the family crystal shattered over time goblet by goblet.

Brain-dead my sisters called me, tidying their cuticles.
Flat-chested my brothers called me,
trailing my knuckles across their tensed stomachs.

Beatings and advances these hands always struck back at,
though the desire to survive I was at odds with,
discovering victory was bruises nursed in my bedroom.

With these hands I would tangle a man's hair.
With these nails I could scratch out his eyes.
With this hand above my head I bid you goodbye.

I step into traffic.
Light drifts down between glass facades and brownstones,
hangs across my shoulders like an overcoat

that repels rain.
In New York disorder descends randomly,
passes out at the back entrance of any crowded restaurant

or behind the cages of the Bronx Zoo.
Why it shadows forth
at this corner as a woman in a nightdress

I am afraid to guess, suspect only that in this city few strangers
catch the eye twice,
each street giddy with windows overwhelmed

by choices and hidden price tags,
browsers fingering bargains
laid out at subway exits on dirty plastic.

I look back: against the tumult she stands
forlorn as a stalled car with the hood up,
engine seized, convulsed with use.

God knows who may take her place,
waiting for the light to change,
a free hand tensing, untensing in a frayed pocket.

Sabra and Shatila

A thousand stones in a bare field.

A thousand stone
heads
face down in the dried mud.

Each stone a bird
weightless
in a cloudless mind

and shot down at moonrise.

Each stone a fallen

feather, the last
touch of a lover

settled forever
under a layer of grit —

beauty's transformation of death
only the imagination's harvest.

      In Beirut, at twilight,
      a child

      hunched on the bullet-
      pocked
      steps of the Hilton Hotel

      turns a pebble

over and over in her
hands.
By chance the sun

settles

in the sights
of a burned cedar's

crossed branches

the dusk a sudden
blood medallion.

Attitudes Toward Ming

A shallow bowl that never broke,
good for feeding chickens.
The old woman dropped

it on the pawn shop counter,
the lotus puffed up
around its sides remaining

unruffled as it spun,
though it stank of uric acid,
its interior bird-shit white.

Such a white, herringboned
with age;
the woman's face waxy,

yellowed as nicotine.
The broker appraised her
eyes: intensity minted

by forty years of plumping
chickens for the People
in a shed within walking distance of Beijing.

A life among many —
for the woman the bowl contained no history,
the design anonymous in her days.

The broker acquired it for the People,
porcelain curves suggestive
to his fingers as he washed it

in jasmine water, placed it in the sun to dry.
Now it sits in a museum cabinet,
catalogued, nuanced by dust,

a curiosity to disarm the Western press.
It accrues no
translucence from the artificial light.

Tapestry

Unravel this —

three women dancing,
a touch of ruse flushing
their cheeks, their laughter

rising, your eyes widening,
set awhirl by the free
wheel of hands linking

and step lightening.
Can you picture
why this cocoon

of figures blurring
balances like a top on Clio's fingertip
as her hand moves

forward into the metamorphosis
of a candlelit
room full of celebrants

spinning folk songs about
disarmament and human rights?
Just look how these women

spill into a single flesh,
six hands urging three sets of hips.
They pull names from the air

Adam could never twist
his tongue around, so left unsaid.
They are giving birth

to the attitudes we are
reclining in, turning
our heads as we watch

them bound in a reel
we may join threading in step
by step, yet, being men,

can never break.

Suddenly Glancing Up from My Book

after Robin Skelton

All week: sun
dazzled rain.

Outside this
afternoon

window, arbutus
branches spread

like wings out
of the mist.

A leaf breaks loose.
Sunlit it falls,

settles as a rail
might each foot

crossing a pool.
A woman crosses

the lawn
in carnation red

stockings.
The remark of her

heel against
a stone

cast long ago
unlinks from it

in rings as if
the stone were

dropping brightly
through water.

The Thirty-Six Poets of Japan

When you refused
to view the legacy

of the splendid dead
with me I went

alone.
On returning you said

Talk to me.
I did.

I told you of the *kogo*
boxes for incense

and the thirty-six
calm-faced

poets of Japan
seated cross-legged

on banks of cushions,
each one

a lotus folding
back into its seed.

I told you how
the nostrils of a dragon

flared with wintergreen,
how the eyes of a blue

porcelain dog
sparked with jasmine.

I told you how
each poet was lacquered

onto wood
by an unknown craftsman,

how each sage
wore a

moustache
drawn

thin with wisdom.
I told you

of a clay
monk disappearing

into a toothless
grin and a squat *geisha*,

her silk *kabuki* face
upturned

to mine, her lips
parted

for a millennium.
I started

to tell you why
art endures

embraced by the
heart, but

your smoke-filled
eyes flickered

into mine and held
us in silence.

Metropolitan Life

The straw hat I left in a New York restaurant
fit with a difference; without it my eyes
squint at the late summer twilight cutting
down through the ginkgoes lining Fifth —
the brim a screen through which I strained the world.

The high-strung woman with whom I split
a bottle of imported Italian bitters
would lean back in her wrought iron chair
and, on occasion, laugh, hands folded safely in her lap,
the table between us a banquet spread
for those who live on little at the city centre.

That night, for the first time, we walked out
into the explosive dark, the air sentient
with leaves impatient to fall, to unroll romance
like a mine field beneath our feet. On such walks
the heart lifts anchor, veers from port toward the Red Sea.
At that moment Flight 007 took off for Soeul from JFK.

The night before, watching a re-run of *Dallas*,
we wondered yet again who the hell shot JR;
across Manhattan, we, the numb in one another's arms, marvelled
how fate connived to reanimate the machinations of his flesh.
Meanwhile refugees pour through the Khyber Pass;
Somalia burns its emaciated Ethiopian dead.

For seven weeks crowds at the Met milled through
rooms of Edouard Manet; a century earlier
he struggled with the idiosyncrasies of the everyday —
the slope of a woman's back while she took her bath,
a girl in mourning, children at the Tuilleries.
In him alone did we recognize a world,
its brevity held in balance between good and evil.

On the radio this morning Tony Bennett left
his heart in San Francisco, but I would bring
mine back.   There is enough loss.
An airliner is shot down over the Sea of Japan;
people are displaced from this earth by war and starvation.
A man and woman walk past the United Nations
into the night, part, wonder where they are.
Who will recover the print of tiny flowers
she left in a midtown restaurant beneath his hat?

Organizational Problems at the Personal Level

This isn't the time to stare at the reflection
thrown back at her by the Frigidaire:
up all night, her hair (grey at 30) a frenzied maze.
She makes for the door, freeing purse and shoes
from eddies of shed work clothes
awash against the four walls of her studio.

The aroma of coffee is a mnemonic
that keeps her going.

At the corner she picks up a day-old New York *Times*
and the world unfolds
a bit off schedule: shots of the Queen kissing
babies in Beijing, bombs in Paris.
In a sunny cafe window she needn't care
if stocks fall on Wall Street
or if science can at last impregnate men.
Conception, she knows, is difficult no matter who you are,
the consequences more improbable if brought to term.
On an empty stomach she can't connect,
reads Miss Manners until the waiter fills her order.
She asks for an expresso, lights a cigarette,
knows the span of time it takes to burn
is the fuse eroding her
last moments of self-expression
before she takes off, explodes in late to work.

What matters are the nightly debates
recurrent over coffee with friends at Zak's.
Discussion isolates the exact
colour of ripe olives,
the fragrance of Montreal after a night of love,
the socio-economic debasement
of the tea ceremony in post-war Japan.
Experience fleshes out the essentials
variously now, no perspective
a consensus —

all that chic about being
and nothingness no longer in vogue,
absorbed in youth like vitamins
by the small intestine.

Somehow she remains unabashed,
strikes another match under one more
nonchalant cigarette, karmas
burning up as she tilts
her head back to laugh.

Walking home on moonless nights,
she can't hide from herself,
conjures up rapists in ill-lit doorways,
her half-clad body pulled from the Rideau Canal.
Tubes and surgeons work into the night
like astronomers descrying signs
of life around some distant star.
Will they feel her drift further from them?
Will she sense no one ever really cared?
The result: negative patient care outcome,
her body unidentified at the morgue.

The catch is she has reasons to live
and these make her late for work.
It is the midnight calls from the man she loves
(long distance romance at 2/3's off costs her sleep);
the view of the river from her balcony
at dawn, currents dragging
up memories of cocoa
with her dad after the graveyard shift.

Each morning she struggles, knows living for the moment
does not pay the rent.
On the down elevator to work, she's noticed her kind
gather around 9 AM; for them disorder
is not subsistence, these hesitantly dressed
men and women wanting coffee, their hair still wet.

Lazaro Screamed

It was an experiment.
No child can sense

the edge negotiated,
in Miami, between reason and death.

Each remains balanced there,
this one standing

on trial at age five years,
unaware of the dangers imaged

every evening as the city approaches
sleep, Dade County thugs hypothesized at the end

of chaotic hallways, behind doors
exploding open —

this boy's life torn
apart by us who as we circle

in judgement like barrio strays,
nose our young into suburbs

away from the heart's complexity.
He could not have guessed

the impact of a five floor fall
until he heard Lazaro scream,

knew only then that this meant pain.
Seconds before, his hands

rested without malice on Lazaro's waist.
He says they were pretending to be falling stars.

Miracles to wish upon his mother always said —
the fire escape without railing,

the world without focus before them
until that moment a world without end.

S.A.L.T. Talks

The text is disarming,
mysteriously
discreet as it lifts
from its hard silo
somewhere in south Arizona,
lifts up near Stratford-on-Avon,
near Moose Jaw or Bremen,
lifts above Aix-en-Provence.
It carries reasonable
allowance for error
toward Odessa, Riga, or Moscow,
slips clean through
the mind's frayed
net of radar,
its image striking
awe on either
side of the Urals.
A mother takes her child
one more time down to the beach,
and then again,
pointing out each shadow
the clouds burn
into the glassy Black Sea
draining like a breast
south through Hell's Gate.
An old man drying into chaff
struggles with details
of war, the ranks
of his comrades so long ago,
their faces misshapen,
a grandson at his bedside
writing down names,
a hot wind lifting
the foolscap
out of his lap.

Lovers linger a touch
longer each night
down the length of the Volga,
each leaf savoured,
each leaf an explosion
of yellows and reds,
drifting, widely drifting.
That men and women
make love all over Russia
is part of the strategy.
Listening to the missile
sing epithalamiums
over their heads
the intended hurry
home from the food-lines
through the permanent
cold of a winter Murmansk.
Once over the threshold
they fall out
of their clothes
into the eternal
warmth of their beds,
their bodies melting
into sleep absolved
of original sin.
It is agreed
at this point the good
men of the Kremlin
will send pushbutton
thanksgiving to America,
Canada, Great Britain,
and France.

It is October 18th,
seventeen hundred hours
Greenwich Mean Time;
in New York we settle
into our weekly
debate on aesthetics.
Somewhere over Ellesmere
two missives
are meeting in an embrace.

Complacency

It's out of control anyway.
The heart fails, a built-in
obsolescence in its muscle.
The soul shimmers, a holograph,
a Polaroid film projected
unexposed inside the body at birth.
The frames turn forward,
record what the eye lights on
each time it shudders open,
shudders until it breaks down —
the film, become opaque,
cast undeveloped inside
the screen of another body.

Consider what the eye chances:
the same memory: your mother taking
family pictures before she died;
my father driving nails into the back
fence, fingers squashed, leaking blood.
Retrospectives of each massacre
glances up from *Der Spiegel*,
Paris Match, *The Observer*, *Time*,
the charred bodies cropped
by a viewfinder with an opinion
to express, our ethos biased.

Yet we can sit through this matinee
and forget, our longing caught
unexpectedly on an indifferent screen.
Coming out, we encounter friends
grainy against the December light.
At Chock Full of Nuts the windows
are smudged with frost, our hands
warmed by steamy mugs of chocolate.

It is an odd time this, yet an orchestra
limbers up on Bach fugues before
the bag ladies of Rockefeller Center.
Laden Christmas shoppers wash past,
frozen briefly when the cold sun
flashes — an enchanted toddler
makes the cover of the New York *Post*.
Framed by the moment, willingly we
turn our collars against the wind.

Recruits

It's all rhythm and blues, rhythm
and blues, the bus driver says as the bus
skids, almost knocks a small child out
of his mother's lap near the front,
the twists in the route,
the black ice and snowdrifts pure
Muddy Waters or John Coltrane.
The trombone section of the Rideau High School
Marching Band boards at five consecutive stops.
They sit apart with their girlfriends,
all hormones and ache, the slides
that glide so freely back
and forth while the band limbers up,
lie awkward between their knees,
each in a worn, velvet-lined case.

It's all rhythm and blues, they play
along with it in someone's basement
after school, the compact disc
ticklish with digitized notes,
the message so potent there is
no need for a lifetime
to comprehend such improvised pain.
They draw it inside and breath out
slowly, note by risky note,
the oxygen so absolute it enters
the blood benignly, feeds the pleasure
centres of the brain.

It's all rhythm and blues, these
excited bodies and what lies ahead,
tunes exhaled in lusty riffs
during their club circuit debut
in Greenwich Village maybe
or lungs scorched by cyanide gas
in a trench near Kuwait.
Whatever happens, something other
than bad timing will separate them,
success or aggression.
To play rhythm or aim a machine gun
commands accuracy, and breathing

is a skill these boys don't yet question
the value of except when some girl
in History class by accident takes it away.

Aftermath

The republics are falling apart
on the evening news —
Croatia, Slovenia.
I look into your eyes
downcast and trampled
by refugees brought here
via satellite, crossing far
borders drafted by some earlier
less electronic war.
Amazing how such distant
and unnatural auroras soothe
and abhor us in this livingroom
where Serbian missiles above
Zagreb tumble, fade
like catherine wheels into the night.
Last year we celebrated
with friends as we too fell
away from each other.
Our bitterness was never so
beautiful, so public.

Now we look for peace,
and see each other on occasion,
never talk about that quiet
holiday in a walled city we used to plan for,
those ancient, winding streets crushed
underfoot like mosaic.

Instead we live with the aftermath,
follow reports of families
in Dubrovnik who pick through wrecked houses
falling toward the Adriatic.
They piece together
an image of their lives
like the shards of an heirloom.
No matter how much care
is given to the glued
fragments of gold-leaf and enamel,
no one can ignore the congealed mends
where everything touches.
The hurt in your eyes
sometimes wounds deeply.
A torn and yellowed
newswire photograph —
what it recalls,
even when heart-felt,
seldom makes sense.

Karme-Choling

Standing on the low banks of the Connecticut River,
an unseasonable thaw for December eroding them down,
I am caught somewhere between source and mouth
unsure of my bearings. The river, an out-breath
unwound to its end, dissolves its current far out
in Long Island Sound. Yesterday I wandered upstream.
My lungs overwhelmed by the warmth of this valley
wedged between mountains lightened of snow,
I let my thoughts turn back to the New York
I left two days before, then to times earlier,
turning away from the river. I encountered
a slough glazed with debris, fed by a spring,
the water dim with sediment churned up as I waded.
Trees knee-deep in mud blocked my path with branches
snarled in the wind. Near dusk I emerged somewhere
along the broken banks of the Connecticut River.
A muskrat, having found its way through rushes
unstiffening in the warmth of the shore, dove
into the current, unperturbed by my presence.

At Karme-Choling, while others sat in meditation
this morning, I was absorbed by the fire.
Lauchlan joined me beside it. With her heart open
she taught me how to become one with my breath.
Cross-legged beside her, I let it carry me out
to its end, again and again, ignoring the 'in'
each time it crowded back into my lungs: my thoughts
beached without meaning on banks shaped for the flow.
Walking down to this moment cast up somewhere
along the softening banks of the Connecticut River
I glanced back: Karme-Choling, its white buildings
red-trimmed, balanced on a rise trained down to a creek
about to merge with the river. All windows shone,
cleansed from the inside by each breath exhaled.
A figure, about to go in, paused on the steps,
the footprints across what remained of the snow
a calligraphy soon to be effaced by the warmth.
Standing on the gentle banks of the Connecticut River,
for the first time I notice the water runs clear.

Crepusculaire

Four roses, yellow, in a chipped vase.
Cut from branches that anchor loose
slats in a neighbour's collapsing
back fence, these buds puff
out from warm centres
atop four sturdy green stems.

Across them we sit, caught
up in their praxis;
light deepens like a premonition
over the west.
Ferns above us fade
into the breeze,
each breath prehensile,
tickling leaves on each frond
like bars of an xylophone.
Gently each loosens more spores.
Eyes close and we lean
profoundly into that breeze.

Give me your hand.
Lines deepen
with such conviction into its palm.
You run the other
over my face; from the hairline
down to my chin, where you linger
fingers spread, I feel you
do so with purpose.

Below in the garden two cats
that earlier dozed
in our laps, pause
amber-eyed in the tall grass,
tails like antennae, noses pressed
to the wind. The sun completes
its fall from the zenith;
against the last
wisp of red the shape
of a hawk
spirals down to the kill.
The eucalyptus stretches.
Like a fruit picker
testing ripeness
with an eye on the future,
it harvests the pale
half-risen moon.

Our faces soften.

This is the hour we fold up our papers;
night has just started
rinsing the glow off the hills.
One more day's newsprint
apocalypse crinkles
like dry leaves in the wind.

This is the moment we live for,
the world in decline.

Unmanned Space Craft

At first,
when the craft landed we
were amazed

how clean the horizons
were,
converging: the perfect

point of a diamond where the planet's
sun rose, cradled
in the soft nexus of distant hills.

Then the camera-eye shifted.
The arrows
of our controls blinked

in disbelief.
The picture travelling its
billions of miles

was still, was so sharp
we saw lush forest,
angel moss and orchids,

spawn-veined rivers teeming
with what seemed
rainbow trout.

Yet is was so far
away, so much deeper
past the last of the nine

dying planets than
we expected,
their itinerary of stars and dead

moons seen as further
proof of the
craft's pointless titching

through the vacancy
of space
at the speed of light.

But that was before,
before the camera-eye trained
on the endless

green of the sky,
before we saw Earth
treading furiously in its vortex

of mist, before we saw
our sun,
a momentary speck of dust

sifting through the clouds locked
across this planet's
flawless, inescapable surface.

SOCIAL NOTE

Books of poetry, like all creative projects, undergo a strange gestation. *Notes Toward a Family Tree* is no different. In light of my earlier work, especially *Great Men* published by Quarry in 1990, I thought readers might be interested in knowing something of its origins.

The two books grew out of the same body of work written mostly in the 1980s, with newer poems added once the manuscripts, like Siamese twins, were separated. Authors, like parents, so often misunderstand their children. Before the surgery took place, I saw them as one book, whose title, *Comedians in the Same Desire*, seems humorous to me now, given the quite different orientations of the two books. At the time the irony was lost on me, but nevertheless, my intentions were serious. Through this proto-manuscript I wanted to combine an exploration of emergent gay sexuality with an exploration of male/female relationships. However ambitious my plans, such a reconciliation was to elude me, so taking the advise of other poets, I broke the manuscript in two, one completely gay, *Great Men*, and one more heterosexual in its tendencies, *Notes Toward a Family Tree*.

Some readers may be curious to know how a gay writer can write about straight experience. Some gay writers would respond that gay men and lesbians have a detached position in society, one which anthropologists seem to value so much: that of the participant observer. However, that sense of detachment is not one of which gay people are always initially aware, especially early in life. Consequently, some of us pursue values and love objects in harmony with those of our straight brothers and sisters, friends and relatives, under the hopeful if not always perceptive eyes of our parents. Our experience is first hand and not just because we were raised to be straight and to live in a straight world. We remain literate in its culture, even after the acknowledgement of our true nature. For some, acceptance occurs in adulthood, often after establishing straight lives with pasts rich in affairs with the opposite sex, children, and spouses, pasts which some unfortunately want to forget. For me, the publication of this book represents a willingness to remember; and, in some small way, I hope it can also represent the collective memory of other gay men and lesbians who once lived, happily, as husbands and wives, or simply as lovers. All too often straight and gay cultures alike question the authenticity of this earlier life.

But *Notes Toward a Family Tree* is about many more things than the love that may or may not exist between men and women, so I don't wish to skew the book entirely by what I have just said. However, I could not allow myself to publish this book without acknowledging its relationship with the one preceding it and with who I am and what I am currently writing.

ACKNOWLEDGEMENTS

Thanks goes to the following journals where some of these poems originally appeared, sometimes in slightly different forms: *Arc*, *Athanor*, *Anthos*, *Canadian Literature* , *Dandelion*, *Descant*, *Event*, *The Fiddlehead*, *Grain*, *Greenfield Review* (U.S.A.), *Mamashee*, *Museum Quarterly*, *New Quarterly*, *Prairie Fire*, *Prospice* (U.K.), *Queen's Quarterly*, *University of Windsor Review*, *Wascana Review*, *Waves*, *West Coast Review*, *Westerly* (Australia).

"Now That Hiroshima is Past Us," "The Thirty-Six Poets of Japan," and "Unmanned Space Craft" appeared in *The Inner Ear*, Gary Geddes, ed., Quadrant Editions, 1982. "Suddenly Glancing Up from My Book" was reprinted in *Skelton at 60*, Barbara Turner, ed., The Porcupine's Quill, 1986. "At the Delta's Edge," "In the Year of," and "The Moabitess" were awarded the Patricia Hackett Prize for Poetry from the University of Western Australia in 1986. "Straits of Juan de Fuca," "At The Delta's Edge," "In the Year of," and "Attitudes Toward Ming" were collected in *Capital Poets: An Ottawa Anthology*, Colin Morton, ed., Ouroboros Press, 1989. "Topographics" and "Organizational Problems at the Personal Level" were finalists in the League of Canadian Poets' 1989 National Poetry Contest and appeared in *More Garden Varieties*: Aya Press/The Mercury Press, 1989. "Recruits" appeared in *A Discord of Flags: Canadian Poets Write about the Persian Gulf War*, Steven Heighton, Peter Ormshaw, and Michael Redhill, eds., 1992. "Vancouver Gothic" was reprinted in *Symbiosis*, Girol Books, 1992. "Housebound" has been collected in *When Is a Poem*, Pembroke Press, 1993.

The quotation opening the book is from Charles Wright's *The Southern Cross* Random House, 1981. Phyllis Webb's "I Can Call Nothing Love" from *Selected Poems*, Talonbooks, 1971 is quoted in "The Centrepiece." The epigram attributed to Elizabeth Smart at the beginning of "Saltspring" is taken from an interview she gave *Books in Canada* in 1982.

Thanks to Blaine Marchand for giving me the original idea for the book. Thanks as well to Nadine McInnis for her help in the selection and arrangement of the poems, and to Neile Graham and James Gurley for their further refinements. Thanks also to the Ontario Arts Council and John Flood at Penumbra for much welcome financial assistance in 1988 through the Writers' Reserve.

"The Centrepiece" is dedicated, with much love, to my sister, Pam, "Notes Toward a Family Tree" to Alison Beaumont, "Heavenly Bodies" to Owen and Nadia Fairbairn, and "Housebound" to Tom McKay.